50: THE AGE OF WHEEZIN'

ILLUSTRATED BY KEVIN AHERN

SHOEBOX GREETINGS
(A tiny little division of Hallmark)

Published in the United States of America
by Hallmark Cards, Inc.

ISBN: 0-87529-706-4

PRINTED IN THE UNITED STATES OF AMERICA.

WEED WHACKER

REMOTE CONTROL

GARAGE DOOR OPENER

RIDING MOWER

POWER SCREW-DRIVER

POWER RECLINER

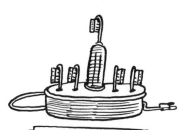

ELECTRIC TOOTHBRUSH

SNOWBLOWER

EXERCISE MACHINES FOR THE 50-YEAR-OLD.

IF YOU GIVE A 50-YEAR-OLD A BOOK THAT POKES FUN AT HIS AGE, HE IS MOST LIKELY TO FIND IT...

A. FUNNY.

B. INSULTING.

C. LYING OPEN ON HIS CHEST WHEN HE WAKES UP.

TOP TEN WAYS TO TELL iF THE DRIVER OF THE CAR iN FRONT OF YOU iS 50

10 "I BRAKE FOR BiNGO" BUMPER STICKER.

9 LOOSE CURB FEELER KEEPS SENDING SPARKS SHOOTING UP OFF THE HiGHWAY.

8 CAR PHONE HAS A TWO-PiECE RECEiVER WiTH A BELL-SHAPED MOUTHPiECE.

7 PERPETUALLY FLASHiNG TURN SiGNAL.

6 VAGUE SOUND OF POLKA TUNE WAFTING UP THROUGH THE SUNROOF.

 5 WHEN CARS COME UP BEHIND HIM DOING 50, HE WAVES THEM PAST.

 **4** WHEN THE DRIVERS OF THE CARS HE WAVES PAST GIVE HIM THE FINGER, HE SMILES AND WAVES.

 **3** MUDFLAPS.

 2 PERSONALIZED PLATE: GEEZER.

AND THE NUMBER ONE WAY TO TELL:

YOU CAN'T SEE DRIVER'S HEAD OVER BACK OF CAR SEAT.

WHAT DOES THIS PiCTURE iLLUSTRATE?

Ⓐ A 50-YEAR-OLD WiTH A REALLY iMPORTANT QUESTION.

Ⓑ A 50-YEAR-OLD BEING ROBBED.

Ⓒ A 50-YEAR-OLD'S ENTiRE AEROBiCS WORKOUT.

A COURTROOM FULL OF 50-YEAR-OLDS.

DRIVING TIPS FROM THE 50-YEAR-OLD:

TEN FAVORITE WESTERNS OF 50-YEAR-OLDS:

1. THE MAN WHO LOVED CATNAPPING"

2. ROOSTER HEARTBURN

3. VERY PALE RIDER

4. A FISTFUL OF VITAMINS

5. THE MILD BRUNCH

6. SHAME

7. FOR A FEW HAIRS MORE

8. MY BIG ELDORADO

9. THE INSIGNIFICANT SEVEN

10. FORT APATHY

WHERE'S THE WORST PLACE TO BE WHEN YOU SEE A 50-YEAR-OLD DRIVING?

(A) IN THE CAR AHEAD OF HIM.

(B) IN THE CAR BEHIND HIM.

(C) IN THE CAR WITH HIM.

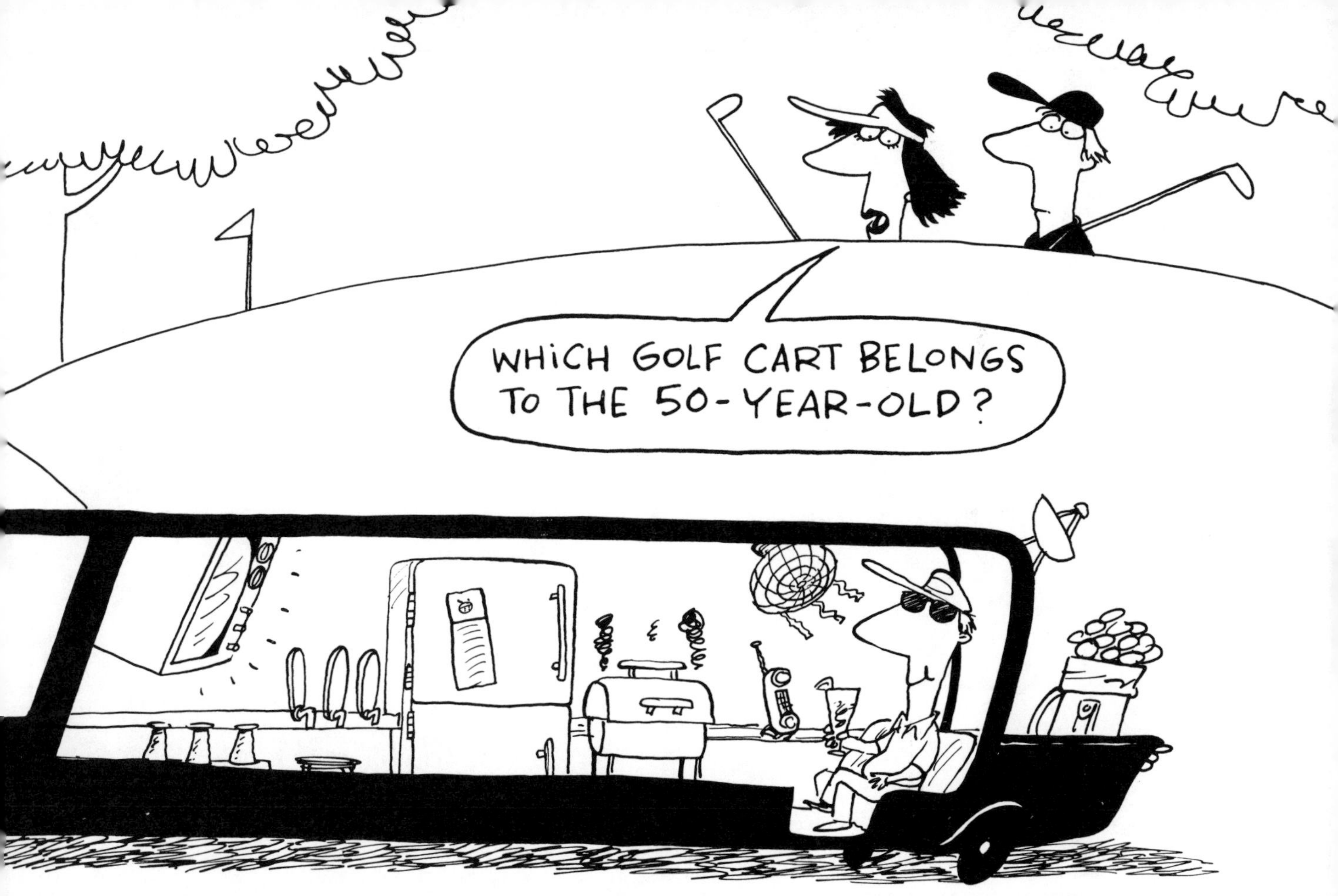
WHICH GOLF CART BELONGS TO THE 50-YEAR-OLD?

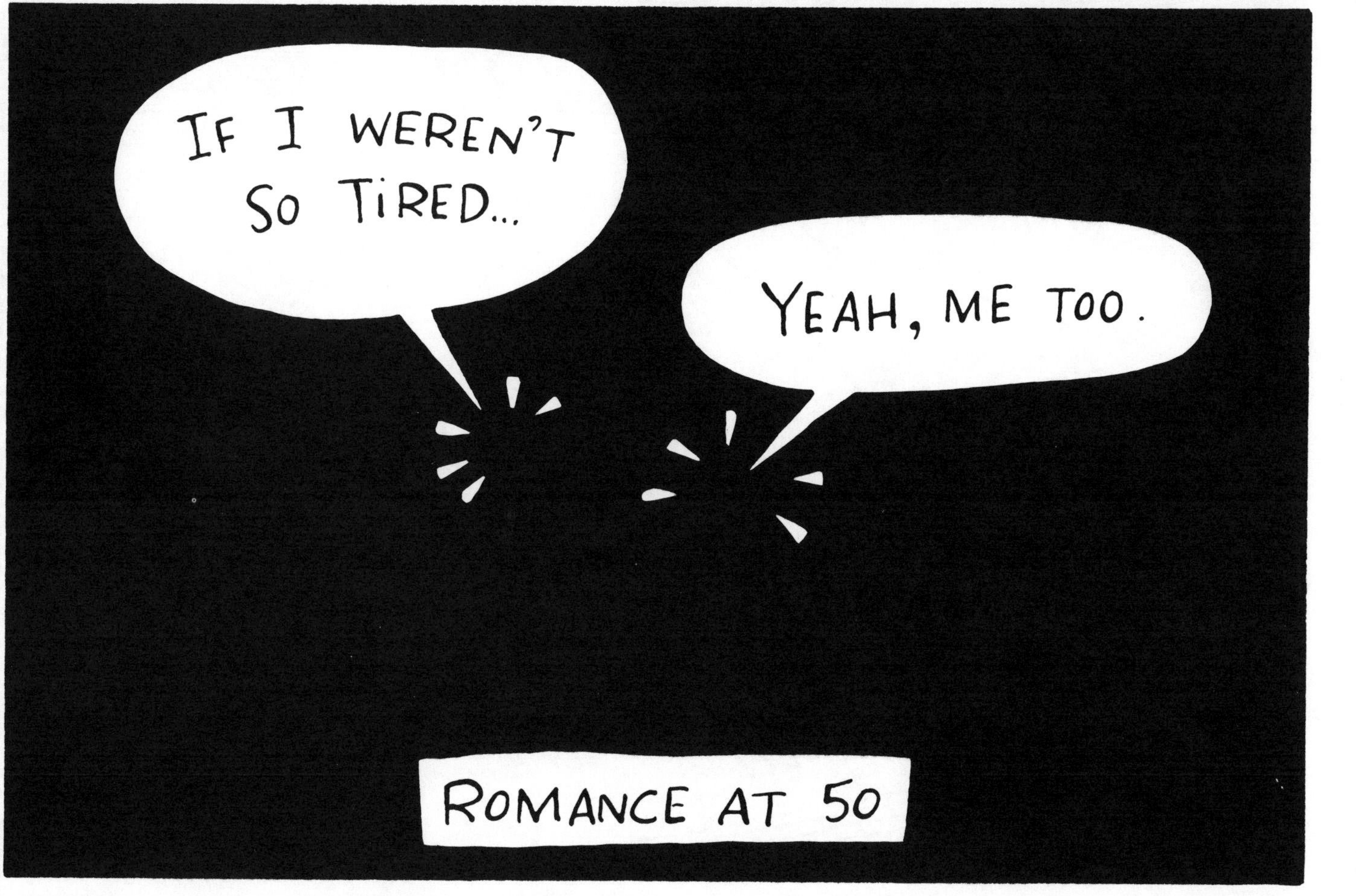
IF I WEREN'T SO TIRED...
YEAH, ME TOO.
ROMANCE AT 50

A TYPICAL CONVENTION FOR 50-YEAR-OLDS.
Hi, MY NAME IS
TAKE ONE
A TYPICAL CONVENTION FOR 50-YEAR-OLDS.
TODAY'S SCHEDULE
5-7 a.m. COFFEE and ROLLS (If you want to get up earlier, you can.)
7-9 a.m. COMPLAIN ABOUT ROOM (a roundtable discussion)
9-Noon OPEN COMPLAINING
12-2 p.m. LUNCH (all-you-can-eat buffet)
2-3 p.m. COMPLAIN ABOUT LUNCH
3-4 p.m. NAP I
4-5 p.m. RECALLING THINGS THAT WERE BETTER
5-6 p.m. NAP II (NAP I a prerequisite)
6-8 p.m. DINNER AND WRAP-UP COMPLAINTS
8:15 p.m. LIGHTS OUT!

WHICH TOURIST IS 50?
HOW AWE-INSPIRING!
OVER 60 STORIES HIGH!
MY ARCHES ARE KILLING ME...

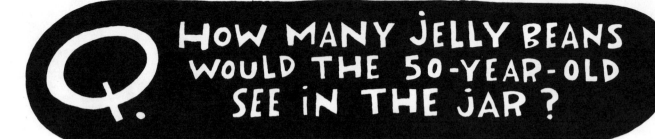

Q. HOW MANY JELLY BEANS WOULD THE 50-YEAR-OLD SEE IN THE JAR?

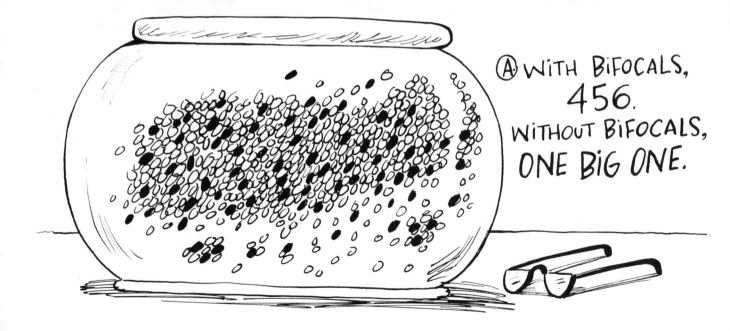

A. WITH BIFOCALS, 456. WITHOUT BIFOCALS, ONE BIG ONE.

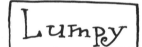

Ouchy

Crabby

Baldy

Grouchy

Saggy

4 THINGS THAT DELIGHT A 50-YEAR-OLD:

① A CAKE WITH LESS THAN 50 CANDLES.

② FINDING A NEIGHBOR KID WITH A NEAT HAIRCUT WHO DOES A GOOD JOB OF MOWING THE LAWN FOR LESS THAN THE PREVAILING WAGE.

③ WAKING UP BEFORE THE END OF AN EXCITING GAME.

④ WAKING UP BEFORE THE END OF AN EXCITING THREE MINUTES OF PASSION.

A Nursery Rhyme for 50-year-olds.

Humpty-Dumpty sat on a wall,
Humpty-Dumpty had a great fall...
But it was okay, because
Humpty had that insurance
you can get for just
pennies a day.

ARE YOU 50? TAKE THIS SIMPLE TEST.

What is the meaning of the drawing below?

(A) THE "PEACE" SIGN.

(B) THE SYMBOL FOR "VICTORY."

(C) THE NUMBER OF FINGERS YOU CAN STILL MOVE WITHOUT EXPERIENCING NAGGING DISCOMFORT.

A 50-YEAR-OLD BUYS JEANS.
DO YOU HAVE ANYTHING LOOSER THAN "LOOSE FIT?"

TRUE OR FALSE:

50-YEAR-OLDS ARE BETTER GOLFERS.

TOP TEN WAYS A 50-YEAR-OLD ENDS AN ARGUMENT

WHAT'S "OUT" and WHAT'S "IN"

← OUT →   FOR 50-YEAR-OLDS: → IN ←

OUT	IN
JOGGING	JOGGING YOUR MEMORY
FAST FOOD	FAST RELIEF
ROCK and ROLL	ROCKING CHAIRS
RUNNING SHORTS	RUNNING TO THE BATHROOM
SPORTS CARS	SPORTS CREAMS
MARATHONS	MARATHON NAPPING

FIVE MOST MISSED THINGS ABOUT BEING YOUNGER:

1. FOODS THAT MAKE A SOUND WHEN BITTEN INTO.

2. HAIR BLOWING IN THE BREEZE.

3. ORIGINAL TEETH.

4. PANTS WITHOUT ELASTIC.

5. THE CONCEPT OF HOPE.

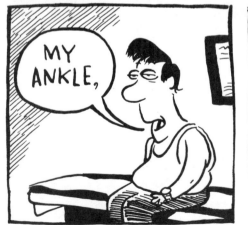

TRUE or FALSE

50-YEAR-OLD MEN HAVE FULL HEADS OF HAIR.

TRUE. JUST NOT THEIR OWN, THAT'S ALL.

LEONARD, A 50-YEAR-OLD, DIDN'T NOTICE THAT SOMEONE HAD TIED HIS SHOELACES TOGETHER UNTIL HE'D BEEN WALKING FOR HALF AN HOUR.

WHAT A 50-YEAR-OLD SAYS :

THINK I'LL CATCH THE LATE NEWS.

YOU WOULDN'T CATCH ME DEAD
IN A SKIRT THAT SHORT!

THANKS, BUT I'M ON A DIET.

I'VE GOT A GAME THIS WEEKEND.

WHAT A 50-YEAR-OLD MEANS:

THINK I'LL SPEND THE NIGHT IN THE RECLINER.

SHE LOOKS TERRIFIC. I HATE HER.

THAT'S RIGHT, IF IT LOOKS GOOD, SMELLS DELICIOUS, AND HAS EVEN THE SLIGHTEST HINT OF FLAVOR -- I CAN'T EAT IT.

I'M GOING TO SPEND THE ENTIRE WEEKEND IN FRONT OF THE TV.

MATCH THE 50-YEAR-OLD'S FOOTWEAR WITH THE APPROPRIATE SOCKS.

① TENNIS SHOES

② LOAFERS

③ SANDALS

④ SLIPPERS

 ① BLACK SOCKS

 ② BLACK SOCKS

 ③ BLACK SOCKS

 ④ BLACK SOCKS

TOP TEN WORDS YOU WILL USE MORE OFTEN NOW THAT YOU'RE 50!

⑩ WHIPPERSNAPPER
⑨ SCIATICA
⑧ BINDING
⑦ OOPS!
⑥ SONNY
⑤ BUFFET
④ OUCH!
③ WHAT?
② BOILED

AND THE NUMBER ONE WORD:

① BINGO!

VULTURES AT 50

FAMOUS PEOPLE AT 50

I REGRET THAT I HAVE SO LITTLE LIFE TO LOSE FOR MY COUNTRY.

NATHAN HALE

I SHALL RETURN, RIGHT AFTER I GO TO THE BATHROOM.

GEN. DOUGLAS MACARTHUR

SIR, I HAVE NOT YET BEGUN TO SHAKE MY FIST.

JOHN PAUL JONES

THERE IS NOTHING TO FEAR, EXCEPT TURNING 50.

FRANKLIN D. ROOSEVELT

SHUFFLE SOFTLY AND CARRY A BIG WALKING STICK.

TEDDY ROOSEVELT

True or False

Even though you're 50, you can still do all the things you did when you were 20.

TRUE. 'COURSE, IT'LL KILL YOU.

R.I.P.
50-YEAR-OLD

A COMMON BUMPER STICKER FOR 50-YEAR-OLDS.

WRITTEN BY

CHRIS BRETHWAITE,
BILL BRIDGEMAN,
CHERYL GAINES,
BILL GRAY,
ALLYSON JONES,
KEVIN KINZER,
MARK OATMAN,
DEEANN STEWART,
DAN TAYLOR,
AND
MYRA ZIRKLE.